SUMMARY GUIDE:

Dr. Gundry's Diet Evolution:

Turn Off the Genes That Are Killing You and Your Waistline By Dr. Steven Gundry

The Mindset Warrior Summary Guide

The
Mindset
Warrior

Table of Contents

Introduction..6

Setting The Stage..8

Chapter 1 – Your Genes..10

Chapter 2 – You Are What You Eat..13

Chapter 3 – Changing Your Genetic Messaging..20

Chapter 4 – Diet Overview: Changing The Messages You Send Your Genes........22

PHASE 1 – The Teardown..45

Chapter 5 – The First Two Weeks...46

Chapter 6 – Foods to Avoid..50

Chapter 7 – The Teardown Continues..54

Chapter 8 – Setting In..61

PHASE 2: The Restoration..66

Chapter 9 – The Beginning...67

Chapter 10 – Exercise...70

PHASE 3: Longevity...73

Chapter 11 – Raw Food Benefits..74

Chapter 12 – Beyond Diet..77

Meal Implementation...80

Chapter 13 – Meal Plans & Recipes...81

Conclusion...83

BONUS:...84

Hi there! Be Sure to Stick Around to the End for a FREE BONUS.

My gift to you; as a special thank you for purchasing this book.

-The Mindset Warrior

MW Summary Guide Disclaimer

This summary guide is in no way associated with and endorsed by Dr. Steven Gundry. This publication is not intended to replace the original work. This publication is a unique summary guide of the original book, and is intended for informational purposes only. It includes some the main ideas, and quotes from the book along with unique commentary. All quotes from the book are properly referenced.

You are encouraged to purchase the original version; if you have not already. This publication has been presented solely for educational & informational purposes as a reference. While best efforts have been made in preparing this book; the author and publisher make no representations or warranties merchantability or fitness of use for a particular purpose. Neither the author, nor the publisher shall be held liable or responsible to any person or entity with respect to any loss or incidental or consequential damages caused, or alleged to have been caused, directly or indirectly, by the information contained herein.

Neither the author, nor the publisher shall be liable for any physical, psychological, emotional, financial, or commercial damages, including, but not limited to, special incidental, consequential, or other damages. You are responsible for your own choices, actions, and results. References are provided for informational purposes only and do not constitute endorsement of any websites or other sources. Readers should be aware that the websites listed in this book may be subject to change.

Introduction

In this Mindset Warrior Summary Guide we cover the main topics discussed in "Dr. Gundry's Diet Evolution". This book is intended to supplement your reading and be an easy reference guide. You are encouraged to purchase the original book if you have not already.

The difference between this guide and the actual book is that we don't go into the lengthy stories and repetition that most books often do. Instead we share each principle, explain its reasoning, and then provide advice on how you can apply each to your own life in order to lose weight, improve your health, and promote longevity.

As I always say, the original books are great to read because they provide a lot of examples. This repetition can help to embed the lessons into your psyche. That being said, stripping these lessons down to their core will help you to focus on the things that really matter. As I'm sure we can agree, time is also very valuable. I am all about maximizing time.

The Mindset Warrior summaries are here to support your journey toward a resilient mindset. **www.mindsetwarrior.com**

Setting The Stage

"Dr. Gundry's Diet Revolution" starts with introducing the understanding that certain issues we've come to accept as normal are actually quite preventable.

Ex: inflammation, depression, acid reflux, weight gain, high blood pressure, etc.

Dr. Gundry purports that we would not have to experience these illnesses if we'd just adjust our lifestyle in a way that turns off our "killer genes".

He explains that the diet we are genetically programmed to eat doesn't promote our health and longevity. The goal of our genes is to reproduce in order to survive, but their pursuit often works to inhibit our survival. The Diet Evolution is all about gaining an understanding of your genetic code, and adjusting your behaviors in a way that activates the health promoting genes, and deactivates the destructive ones.

Dr. Gundry's Credentials:

- over 30 years experience as a heart surgeon and researcher.

- former professor of surgery and pediatrics in cardiothoracic surgery at Loma Linda University School of Medicine.

- inventor of Gundry Retrograde Cardioplegia Cannula *(a device to aid the heart muscle during open heart surgery)*

- a fellow of the American Surgical Association

- 1 of 20 to test an artificial heart

- one of the first to use robots in operation

- the first to perform heart valve operations through 2 inch holes

- over 300 articles published

He briefly explains his personal history with obesity, hypertension, and insulin resistance. When he was dealing with those things he was adhering to what is commonly identified as healthy lifestyle behaviors: going to the gym, eating "healthy" and consuming diet products. In trying to solve his health problems he began adhering to a diet he says is based on the principles of his Diet Evolution protocol.

The first part of the book discusses how our genes work, and how to reprogram them through diet, and the rest of the book discusses a 3 phase program to see results within 3 months.

The 2 main points you should takeaway from the book is how to lose weight through diet and how to promote your longevity.

Chapter 1 – Your Genes

Genes are the operational manual of every function in the body. They will turn on or off depending on what they have determined is most conducive to their survival. Sometimes what promotes their survival does so at the expense of our body. With this in mind, it's important to understand how they work in order to lose weight and promote longevity.

Genes Turn On or Off Based On:

- hormones

- neurotransmitters

- food

- and a variety of other factors..

3 Main Goals of Genes

(1) Finding and conserving energy

In the past, food was not always available to us; while at the same time, low energy due to a lack of nutrition made us more susceptible to predators. These two factors threatened our genes survival, thus making them compelled to conserve energy at all costs. This is why we are compelled to eat high calorie foods and be sedentary.

(2) Avoid pain

Being in pain signals to our genes a decrease in our chances for survival.

(3) Find pleasure

Our genes get pleasure from inactivity and overindulgence. Lifestyle factors that contribute to activating our pleasure seeking killer genes include:

- over-eating

- over-exercising

- inactivity

- smoking

Food and other substances became more available with the introduction of industrialization; as a result, we provided an environment where our genes can get what they want with little effort.

The Western Diet

Research shows that the adoption of a diet full of refined carbohydrates leads to many of the diseases that we face today. These diseases are our body's response to the reproduction of genes. Genes want you to have lot of stored energy (fat) and they want to reproduce (hyper-sexuality). Its important to understand that many behaviors we find compulsive are a response to our genes desire to proliferate.

Cardiovascular Disease

According to the CDC, about 1 in every 4 deaths are a result of cardiovascular disease. In the struggle for survival, your genes conveniently blocks the brain and heart arteries to produce heart attacks and strokes. The blockage of those two arteries create the most impact to effectively slow you down in order to gain control of your bodily function.

Over The Counter Drugs

Over the counter drugs can be effective treatments, but keep in mind that they can train us to blind ourselves to identifying the cause of our ailments, and instead to just treat the symptom.

Chapter 2 – You Are What You Eat

In this chapter Dr. Gundry walks us through the history of the human diet in order to help us understand what led up to our modern diet, and its resulting diseases.

Evolution of The Human Diet

Our diets use to be micro-nutrient rich and calorie sparse. We use to get most of our micro-nutrients from consuming herbivores. Micro-nutrients help with a variety of biological processes in the body, and they direct our genes to turn on or off.

Nutrient Deficiency

Overtime we lost our ability to make B12; and while most animals can create their own vitamin C, humans cannot. Dr. Gundry purports that we have come accustomed to this reality, but it might not have to be that way if we learn how to turn on the correct genes.

Our modern diet has shifted from low calorie micro-nutrient rich foods to high calorie micro-nutrient deficient foods. We now consume more plants than we use to. This is partially due to the fact that most meat these days are raised on grains instead of plants, so in order to meet our micro-nutrient requirements we have to look elsewhere.

NOTE: It is believed by some researchers that the cause of overeating is the body trying to meet its micro-nutrient needs.

The Agricultural Revolution

The domestication of animals started about 10,000 years ago. It required more energy expenditure, but it allowed for easy access to high calorie foods, and it protected us from over-hunting being a threat to our food supply.

The Domestication of Grains

Unfortunately, the energy requirements for maintaining animals didn't satisfy our genetic desire to conserve energy. With this being the case, the invention of processes that lessened our energy expenditure became more intriguing. This intrigue resulted in the domestication of grains.

The Cost of Processing Grains

Grains were introduced so quickly into our diet that its likely our bodies were not prepared to handle them. The introduction of white flower and the resulting increase in disease forced the government to require the process of enriching these foods. Unfortunately the new regulation did not acknowledge the fact that grains; ones processed, easily spike our blood sugar and thus in excess leads to fat storage.

Learning From Wild Animals

It is important to note that the condition of "overweight" does not exist in the wild, with the exception of animals that hibernate in the winter. This observation is believed to be the case due to their:

- adequate stores of body fat

- micro-nutrient rich diets

- adherence to their circadian rhythm

The Nature of Plants

Like any organism, plants what to reproduce their genes. In order to protect their survival, they have a way of producing toxins that help to deter animals from eating them.

NOTE: Dr. Gundry states that these toxins are the reason dogs will chew on new grass, but will only eat mature grass when they want to throw up.

Our increase in our consumption of plants has forced our genetic code to find a defense mechanism to process the toxins that are frequently found in plants.

NOTE: Dr. Gundry dives more into this in his latest book, "The Plant Paradox"

How Plants Manipulate Your Genes

When you consume glucose, your insulin levels rise and your body releases a hormone called leptin in order to signal that it has eaten enough. When we consume fruit glucose (i.e. fructose), this process is altered; insulin rises slower, and leptin isn't released. As a result we are encouraged to keep eating due to a lack of satiety. This process served us in times of food scarcity where it was useful to get in a lot of calories at one time in order to prepare for less opportunities for food during the winter seasons, but of course in today's society of food abundance, this reality does not serve us.

NOTE: Our intestinal tract contains compounds that act as fertilizer. Plants that have eatable seeds act to lure in predators in order to proliferate.

Anti-Nutrients

Anti-nutrients are the survival mechanism for plants that don't produce toxins and/or have sweet tastes. Legumes are one of these plants. They have a nutrient called phytates that negatively affects the absorption of other nutrients in the process of digestion.

Anti-nutrients have the ability to serve our bodies positively too because they act to prevent a conducive environment for cell proliferation. These toxic nutrients can help to inhibit the growth of cancer cells for example. They can also act as a mild stressor to activate certain genes that promote longevity.

Vegetables VS. Meat

In societies where meat consumption is low, humans tend to be smaller in size and reproduce later. Comparatively, in societies where meat consumption is high, humans tend be larger and reproduce more.

The correct dose of plant consumption can help with longevity, but at the same time the addition of the heat production the results from breaking down meat can help with weight maintenance; though it does accelerate aging.

The Job of Insulin

- Deliver nutrients to the cells in order to produce energy

- Convert excess glucose into body fat

- Produce cell growth

The modern frequency at which we have consumed food has led to constantly elevated insulin levels. As a result we've made our bodies very efficient at storing fat.

Sweet Deception

We are genetically programmed to seek sweet tastes because sweet foods are often higher in calories and activate the pleasure centers of the brain.

For this reason, its important to have rules around your consumption of sweet tasting foods.

The Role of Dietary Fat

We are compelled to eat fat because fat has higher calories. Higher calories means more energy and less expenditure for our genes. Dietary fat also plays a role in the absorption of Vitamin, A, E , and K, among other fat soluble vitamins.

NOTE: The combination of sugar and fat create the perfect signals for the body to store fat.

Omega 3 and Omega 6

These two essential fatty acids control most of our hormonal system. Omega 3s work to activate anti-inflammatory hormones and omega 6s work to activate inflammatory hormones. It is the relationship between these two hormones that gives the body homeostasis *(a stable state of being).*

Omega 3 can be found in:

mackerel, salmon, and sardine

Omega 6 can be found in:

grains and some seeds

As our diets have evolved, our ratio of omega 3 to 6 have shifted. We now consume a high omega 6 and low omega 3 diet. This is due to the decline in vegetables and grass fed meat consumption, and our increase in grains and grain fed meat.

NOTE: low presence of omega 3 has been associated with depression

Salt & The Body

The body needs salt in order to carry out many hormonal processes. Because our bodies are made up of 70% salt water, we are compelled to find salty foods. We excrete salt in sweat, so the compulsion to consume continues with physical exertion.

Chapter 3 – Changing Your Genetic Messaging

Our genes compel us to consume that which in our modern world results in health problems and weight gain. We are programmed to consume more sugar, fat, and salt; all of which alert our genes to conserve energy *(i.e. fat gain)*

Reprogramming Our Genetic Messaging

Many people believe they are doomed to their genes, but genes are not as uncontrollable as they are often given credit.

The key to gaining control over our bodies comes down to feeding our genes in ways that challenges them to adhere to promoting our survival, and not just theirs.

By engaging in the "correct" behaviors, we train our genes to activate the information necessary to maintain a healthy weight, and compel us to eat foods that serve our survival.

Forming New Habits

- Sweet foods should be avoided *(even artificial sweeteners)*

- Weigh yourself every morning *(preferably a scale with body weight measurements)*

- Stop weighing your food

In order to effectively form new habits you have to get rid of the myths that you've frequently heard and adopted. It has been said that 6 weeks of continuous practice will make a new habit second nature.

Here are some things to understand before moving forward:

- plants produce chemical toxins in order to deter predators

- animal genes have evolved with plant phytochemicals

- the presence or absence of phytochemicals in cells regulates cellular dysfunction.

- plant compounds are good for you because their bad for you and as result they help to produce hormesis.

Hormesis according to the Merriam Webster dictionary is: a phenomenon of dose-response relationships in which something that produces harmful biological effects at moderate to high doses may produce beneficial effects at low doses

- modern processed foods are "good for you" because they serve your genes' survival by activating your energy storage hormones.

- modern fats that tend to be made up of mostly omega 6 help promote inflammation and depression

Chapter 4 – Diet Overview: Changing The Messages You Send Your Genes

Chapter 4 dives into Dr. Gundry's Dietary Protocol

DISCLAIMER: always consult with a physician before starting a new protocol.

Dr. Gundry advises that you have the following tests performed before embarking on his protocol in order to test the effectiveness after successfully completing the phases of his diet.

• Fasting glucose level

• Hemoglobin A1C

• Fasting insulin level

• Fasting lipid panel *(preferably with fractions of LDL and HDL, lipoprotein(a) or Lp(a), Apo B, Lipo-PLA2)*

• Homocysteine

• Fibrinogen

• C-reactive protein (CRP)

The Objectives of the 3 Phases of The Gundry Diet

Dr. Gundry's diet takes you through 3 phases that varies the types and quantity of food you consume, and exercise that you do.

Message 1: There is no need to store fat for future famine AKA The Teardown Phase

- Consume high protein foods about the size of your palm

- Consume as much vegetables as you desire

- Snack on nuts and seeds twice daily

- Avoid food made of sugar

- Avoid processed foods

Stay on this phase for 6 weeks. Those with the need for more weight loss can stay on it for up to a year.

Message 2: You're not threatening future generations AKA the Restoration Phase

- Increase your vegetable intakes

- Decrease your animal protein intake

- Snack on nuts and seeds twice daily *(add in berries in moderation)*

- Consume small portions of whole grains and legumes if you choose

Stay on this phase for 6 weeks, or until your weight normalizes.

<u>Message 3: Staying Alive = Genetic Proliferation AKA the Longevity Phase</u>

- Consume food with high micro-nutrients but are calorie sparse *(i.e. vegetables)*

- Avoid high caloric foods *(whole grains, legumes, etc.)*

- Reduce animal protein

NOTE: This phase continues indefinitely

Exercise

Dr. Gundry stresses that a cardio focused exercise regime mimics the lifestyle of "low-tier" animals; instead we should adjust for an exercise plan that is more constructive to our genes.

NOTE: He discusses more about this in Ch.10

Supplementation

Supplementation should be thought of as health insurance. Because we consume less variety of plants, we need to use supplements to get our adequate micro-nutrient intake.

NOTE: our ancestors ate up to 200 different types of plants. In today's society that's likely impossible to mimic.

Dr. Gundry's "Friendly Foods" to Eat

NOTE: This is the exact list provided in "Dr.Gundry's Diet Revolution"

Meat *(ideally grass fed)*

- Beef filet, flank steak, stew meat, ground sirloin, round steak, jerky

• Lamb

• Pork tenderloin, ham, Canadian bacon, prosciutto *(but no slab bacon)*

• Wild game, venison, bison

Poultry *(preferably free-range)*

• Chicken

• Cornish game hen

• Duck

• Goose

• Turkey

• Turkey "bacon"

• Turkey and chicken cold cuts, preferably sliced and not processed parts

• Wild poultry

Fish *(preferably wild, not farm raised)*

• Alaskan halibut

• Anchovies

• Freshwater bass

• Hawaiian fish *(such as ono, mahimahi, opakapaka)*

• Mackerel

• Salmon, preferably Alaskan; also canned and smoked salmon

• Sardines

• Shellfish *(including crab, lobster, squid, calamari, shrimp, scallops, clams, and mussels)*

• Trout

• Whitefish and perch *(preferably from Lake Superior)*

• Yellowtail and albacore tuna; also canned tuna

Meat Protein Substitutes

- 1 cup of cheese, yogurt, or unsweetened soy or almond milk

- 1 oz of aged cheese

- 2 - 3 eggs per day

- 1/2 cup black soybeans or edamame

- 1 pk of tofu noodles

<u>Dairy products (and substitutes)</u>

FRESH CHEESES

• Farmer cheese (1 cup)

• Feta cheese (½ cup)

• Low-fat cottage cheese (1 cup)

• Mozzarella cheese, water packed (½ cup)

• Ricotta (1 cup)

AGED CHEESES

• Asiago

• Bleu cheese

• Cheddar

• Goat cheese (any kind)

• Gruyère

• Pecorino Romano

- Parmigiano-Reggiano

- Swiss

OTHER DAIRY

- Almond milk (plain or flavored, unsweetened only)

- Eggs (preferably omega-3, free-range preferred)

- Kefir

- Soymilk (plain or flavored, unsweetened only)

- Yogurt (plain, unsweetened only)

Soy and related protein sources

- Black soybeans

- Edamame

- Seitan (warning, this is wheat gluten)

- Tempeh

- Tofu (firm only)

- Tofu shirataki noodles

Vegetables

You can eat as much of the following as you wish.

NOTE: 3-4 cups of raw leafy vegetables equate to 1 cup of cooked vegetables

LEAFY GREENS

• Arugula

• Beet greens

• Chard

- Collards

• Dandelion

• Endive

• Escarole

• Kale

• Lettuce, including romaine, Boston, and all red and green lettuces

• Mustard greens

• Purslane

• Radicchio

• Spinach

- Turnip greens

- Watercress

OTHER VEGETABLES

Eat as many of these vegetables as you'd like with the exception of pumpkin.

- Artichokes

- Bamboo shoots

- Beans (string, green, yellow)

- Bean sprouts

- Beets (raw only)

- Bok choy

- Broccoli and broccoli rabe

- Brussels sprouts

- Cabbage (napa, Chinese, green and red)

- Capers

- Carrots (raw only)

- Cauliflower

- Celery

- Chayote (vegetable pear)

- Chicory

- Cucumbers (including pickles)

- Fennel

- Garlic

- Ginger root

- Herbs (cilantro, basil, mint, sage, oregano, parsley, rosemary, thyme, etc.)

- Jícama

- Kohlrabi

- Mushrooms

- Olives

- Onions, shallots, scallions, chives

- Peppers (hot, such as jalapeño)

- Peppers (sweet bell, all colors)

- Pumpkin (up to 1 cup a day)

- Radishes (including daikon)

- Sugar snap peas, snow peas (but not shelled peas)

- Summer squash (patty pan, yellow crookneck, zucchini)

- Water chestnuts

NOTE: some root vegetables like beets and carrots are good to have raw, but their full of sugar which result in a quick insulin spike when cooked.

<u>Oils</u>

Oils work great as a replacement for salad dressing. You can cook with some of them, but not all oils are suitable for cooking due to their smoke point. Here is a list covering the smoke points of the most common oils:

<u>https://jonbarron.org/diet-and-nutrition/healthiest-cooking-oil-chart-smoke-points</u>

- Canola oil

- Flaxseed oil (do not heat)

- Grapeseed oil

- Hempseed oil (do not heat)

- Macadamia nut oil

- Olive oil *(extra-virgin only, preferably unfiltered and cold pressed)*

- Sesame oil *(both plain and Asian roasted)*

- Tahini *(in small amounts only)*

- Walnut oil *(do not heat)*

Condiments

Use condiments sparingly. Avoid ones made with sugar, artificial sweeteners, and corn syrups.

- A.1. Steak Sauce

- Fish sauce (nam pla)

- Lemon and lime juice

- Mustard (without honey or sugars)

- Salsa (preferably fresh)

- Salt and pepper

- Spices and herbs

- Tabasco and other hot sauces

- Tamari or soy sauce

- Tomato sauce or paste

- Vinegar *(apple cider preferred, or any other type)*

• Worcestershire sauce

<u>Nuts & Seeds</u>

Have at most ¼ cup twice a day of nuts or seeds. Choose the unsalted and raw nuts and seeds *(peanuts are an exception).*

NOTE: avoid sunflower seeds due to their high omega 6 content, avoid cashews because they are high in sugar, and consume nut butters sparingly; up to 2 tablespoons a day.

• Almonds

• Brazil nuts

• Cocoa beans (cocoa nibs) or chocolate with greater than 70 percent cocoa

• Coconut, dried or fresh unsweetened only (very high in calories)

• Flaxseeds (ground)

• Hazelnuts

• Hemp seeds (or powder)

• Macadamias

• Peanut butter and other nut butters

• Peanuts *(unless you're cooking with them, use only roasted peanuts)*

- Pecans

- Pepitas

- Pine nuts *(pignolia)*

- Pistachios

- Pumpkin seeds

- Sesame seeds

- Walnuts

Meal Replacement Powders & Bars

Use these foods occasionally when convenience is needed. Look for brands that are high in protein, low in carbs, and low in artificial sweeteners.

NOTE: artificial sweeteners have been shown to be able to elicit an insulin response.

- Most low-carb protein bars, including:

  - Atkins Advantage

  - Doctor's Carbrite Diet

  - Pure Protein

  - Think Thin

- Most low-carb protein shakes, such as Atkins Advantage and Pure Protein

- Hemp protein powder (unsweetened)

- Rice protein powder (unsweetened)

- Soy protein powder (unsweetened)

- Whey protein powder (unsweetened)

Beverages

- Coffee

- Consommé, bouillon, clear broth

- Plain spirits without mixers

- Red wine

- Tea *(black, green, white, and herbal)*

Dr.Gundry's "Unfriendly Foods" to Avoid

<u>Vegetables</u>

The vegetables listed below contain starches that quickly turn into sugar. Some of them can be eaten raw, but they should be avoided when cooked.

• Beets (cooked)

• Carrots (cooked)

• Corn (cooked)

• Peas (shelled)

• Root vegetables (parsnips, turnips, rutabagas, celery root)

• Sweet potatoes

• Winter squash (Hubbard, acorn, butternut, and others)

• Yams

<u>"White Foods"</u>

While some are actually white in color, the term "white" is mostly used to indicate processed.

• Artificial sweeteners *(Equal, Sweet 'n Low, Splenda, etc.)*

• Candy *(including sugar-free)*

- Flour

- Frozen yogurt

- Ice cream

- Mayonnaise

- Milk *(skim, or fat-free, are the worst)*

- "No-added-sugar" foods

- Pasta

- Potatoes

- Ranch dressing

- Rice *(including white basmati and most brown rice)*

- Rice milk

- Saltines

- Soymilk, regular or "lite" *(unsweetened is okay)*

- Sugar

- White bread

<u>"Beige Foods"</u>

• Bagels

• Blended coffee drinks

• Bread *(including flat bread, pita, and whole wheat, whole-grain, and sprouted-grain products)*

• Breaded food *(any kind)*

• Buns

• Cereals *(hot and cold)*

• Chips

• Cookies

• Crackers

• Deep-fried food *(any kind)*

• French fries

• Low-fat processed foods

• Muffins

• Pastry

• Pizza

- Pretzels

- Rolls

- Tortillas *(flour or corn)*

Fruits

- Dates

- Dried fruits of any kind (currants, prunes, blueberries, cranberries, etc.)

- Fruit leather/strips

- Mangos

- Pineapple

- Plantains

- Raisins

- Ripe bananas

- Ripe papayas

- Ripe pears

- Seedless grapes

OTHER FOODS TO AVOID

- Alcohol in a mixed drink, white or rosé wine, beer, malt liquors

- Fruit juice *(all kinds)*

- Honey, molasses, maple syrup, corn syrup, and other sweeteners

- Jam, jellies, preserves, condiments made with sugar

- Jell-O *(including sugar-free Jell-O)*

- Soft drinks, including sugar-free and diet brands

- Vegetable juice *(all kinds)*

Foods to Avoid <u>Initially</u>

<u>"BROWN" FOODS</u>

NOTE: eating these foods will slow your weight loss.

• Amaranth

• Barley

• Brown basmati rice *(from India)*

• Buckwheat *(kasha)*

• Bulgur

• Corn kernels *(fresh and raw only)*

• Farro

• Legumes *(beans such as lentils, lima, garbanzo, navy, pinto, kidney, etc.)*

• Millet

• Oats *(whole or steel-cut, but not old-fashioned or quick oats)*

• Quinoa

• Rye

• Soy/spelt/garbanzo bean flour *(for coating only)*

• Spelt

• Whole wheat berries

• Wild rice

FRIENDLY FRUITS

This list of fruits can be added back after the first 2 weeks in Phase 1, but consuming them will slow weight loss. You can have up to two servings of these fruits a day after reintroducing them.

• Apple *(1 medium)*

• Apricots *(4 fresh)*

• Avocado *(½)*

• Banana—green-tipped only *(1)*

• Blackberries (1 cup)

• Blueberries *(1 cup)*

• Boysenberries *(1 cup)*

• Cherries *(1 cup, about 10)*

- Citrus—oranges, grapefruit, tangerines, tangelos *(one whole, or half a grapefruit)*

- Cranberries *(1 cup)*

- Currants *(1 cup fresh)*

- Grapes—but not seedless ones *(1 cup)*

- Guava—no guava juice *(3 small)*

- Huckleberries *(1 cup)*

- Kiwi (1)

- Kumquats (2)

- Lychees *(1 cup, about 5)*

- Mulberries *(1 cup)*

- Nectarine (1)

- Papaya—green only, in salads (1)

- Passion fruit (1)

- Peach *(1 medium)*

- Pear—firm, not ripe *(1 medium)*

- Plums *(2 small or 1 medium)*

- Pomegranate *(½ cup seeds)*

- Raspberries *(1 cup)*

- Strawberries *(1 cup, about 6)*

- Tomato *(1 medium)*

Restaurant Tips

- Avoid free "carb full" appetizers like bread-sticks.

- Consider eating appetizers and salads, instead of an entrée.

- Replace any rice, potato, or pasta in an entrée with vegetables.

- Order berries for dessert. If they are not available consider splitting a dessert with another person or avoiding it altogether.

PHASE 1 – The Teardown

Chapter 5 – The First Two Weeks

In the first 2 weeks of Phase 1 you want to convince your genes that you are in the "winter season" so it does not need to activate its fat storage mechanism. In order to do this, most of your calories will come from protein and sources listed in the <u>"friendly foods" section from chapter 4</u>. Consume these foods in the portion size of a palm, pair them with leafy greens vegetables, and snack on nuts and seeds.

In the past, a high protein diet made up most of our calories during the winter season. A high protein diet activates the fat burning mechanisms of the body. Protein is the least efficient source of energy and burns 30% of calories in the process of its digestion. This will help you to burn any excess fat stores.

NOTE: Research has shown that when we eat a high protein meal we consume less calories than when we eat a high fat or high carb meal

Losing Weight Quickly

It is normal to see the scale drop quickly in the beginning of your diet. Quick weight loss is often a result of the water loss that results from the release of the water molecule that make up glycogen. Glycogen is the storage form of glucose in the liver.

NOTE: It is normal to lose about 3 -5 lbs of water in the beginning of Phase 1

Greens In Your Diet

Vegetables provide volume in our diet. This works to increase our satiation, while providing us with our micro-nutrient requirements.

Eat as much of the friendly vegetables from Ch. 4 as you want.

Other Rules of Thumbs:

- drink 8 - 10 glasses of water daily

- have a mid morning and mid afternoon snack of 1/4 cup of nuts or seeds

- vary your vegetables

Nuts & Seeds As A Snack:

Dr. Gundry says that snacking on nuts & seed can help prevent the body from resorting to muscle catabolism for fuel. Whole nuts and seeds provide the added benefit of not being completely digestible, which results in the absorption of only 1/3 of their calories.

NOTE: avoid roasted or salted nuts and seeds (besides peanuts) because heating nuts and seeds leads to the oxidization of the nutrients contained in them.

Getting Rid of Sugar Cravings

The author identifies 3 supplements to take to reduce sugar cravings and in combination can help to prevent excessive insulin spikes.

Selenium (200-400 mcg)

Cinnamon (500-1,000 mg 2x daily)

Chromium (400-1,00 mcg)

Beneficial Bacteria

Consuming processed foods sends our intestines chemical signals that inhibit the growth of beneficial bacteria.

Consider taking prebiotics. They work to improve the presence of beneficial bacteria in our gut. Beneficial bacteria aids the absorption of nutrients, lowers your cholesterol, and promotes a healthy immune system.

Some of the <u>friendly vegetables</u> discussed in Chapter 4 that are high in prebiotics are: garlic, onion, leeks, mushroom, asparagus, and artichokes.

Meat Protein Substitutes

- 1 cup of cheese, yogurt, or unsweetened soy or almond milk

- 1 oz of aged cheese

- 2 - 3 eggs per day

- 1/2 cup black soybeans or edamame

- 1 pk of tofu noodles

Chapter 6 – Foods to Avoid

The "unfriendly foods" listed in Chapter 4 can be used as an exact guide book, but consider these 6 points as a shortcut:

- food that are white or beige

- foods containing sugar

- sodas

- alcoholic mixes

- fruit and vegetable juices

- white wines and beers

Beyond the harmful effects to our body, its important to avoid these substances in order to break your compulsion for them.

NOTE: These are foods that are attractive to our genetic survival.

In the first two weeks remove:

- fruits

- whole grains and legumes

- fruits commonly labeled as vegetables *(tomatoes, avocado, eggplant, etc.)*

- cooked root vegetables

Why Milk Should Be Avoided

Mammals are designed to stop drinking milk and develop an intolerance after infancy.

NOTE: 1/3 of the population has a gene that prevents intolerance

Milk contains IGF, a hormone that helps stimulate growth. This growth is nondiscriminatory and as a result can stimulate growth of cancer cells. IGF also spikes insulin, which prevents your body from shutting down its fat storage mechanism.

The Pace of Weight Loss

Toxins are often stored in fat. Losing fat too quickly results in the rapid release of these toxins into your bloodstream. Research has also shown that quick weight loss tends to result in eventual weight relapse.

NOTE: Aim for 1 pound of weight loss a week.

The 5 Supplements for Your Diet

A multivitamin provides the minimum nutritional requirement, but Dr. Gundry recommends these 5 supplements to consider adding to your regimen:

Vitamin E (400 - 2k IU)

- a antioxidant

NOTE: Some research has suggested that doses between 1,600 to 2k IU are needed for effective absorption.

Vitamin C (500 - 1k mg 2x daily)

- repairs collagen, micro-nutrient booster

Magnesium (500- 1k mg)

- helps with muscle contraction and nerve conduction

Folic Acid Along with Other B Vitamins

- regulate biological processes

Troubleshooting

If you find you are not losing weight, start tracking exactly what you eat.

NOTE: women tend to lose body fat slower than males, and males tend to lose belly fat slower than other body parts.

Beyond Two Weeks?

Two weeks is the minimum requirement to stay in the first part of the Teardown phase, but if you are overweight, have diabetes, or other metabolic diseases, you might want to consider staying on this 2 week regimen longer.

Chapter 7 – The Teardown Continues

Now that the first 2 weeks of the Teardown phase is done, the body recognizes it doesn't need to activate its fat storage mechanism because its in the "winter phase". Next we'll begin to slowly evolve the diet so that our bodies understand its in a controlled fed state.

Continue consuming Dr.Gundry's friendly foods and avoid the unfriendly ones.

Adding Fruit Back In

Foods like berries, currants, cherries, red grapes, and plums provide a lot of phytonutrients, which helps to turn on our longevity genes. You can begin introducing them back into your diet after the first 2 weeks. For fruits like apples, citrus fruits, tomatoes, or avocados, limit yourself to at most 2 servings a day. If your weight loss stalls, you'll want to reduce or remove fruit altogether.

NOTE: avoid seedless and dried fruits

Adding Brown Foods Back In

You can add up to 1/2 cup of cooked whole grains or legumes that are brown (refer to Ch.4). You'll still want to avoid the refined carbohydrates from breads and similar foods, andou'll want to weigh your portions until you can comfortably eyeball a 1/2 cup portion size.

NOTE: If you have a lot of weight to lose or are stalling in your weight loss, you'll want to avoid brown foods for now.

Protein to Vegetable Ratio

Begin cutting back on your protein intake and raise your "friendly vegetable" intake. The idea is to decrease caloric density and increase your micro-nutrients.

NOTE: By the end of week 6 you'll want to have your protein portions about half the size of your palm.

Guidelines from The First 2 Weeks to Continue

- Your supplementation

- ¼ cup of nuts mid-morning & mid-afternoon

- 8 - 10 glasses of water per day

Understanding Cholesterol

There is a common myth that dietary cholesterol will raise your blood cholesterol. More and more research is showing that levels of bad cholesterol are almost entirely controlled by the sugar and starches in food.

LDL "Bad" Cholesterol has 7 different kinds.

HDL "Good" Cholesterol has 5 different kinds.

25% of humans carry a gene that codes for the ability to produce a deadly cholesterol labeled lipoprotein(a) (Lp(a).

Statins or dietary changes will not affect levels of Lp(a).

NOTE: People with ancestors from north Europe or the British Isles are more apt to carry this gene

Dr. Gundry recommends that you measure your Lp(a) levels. He claims that his research on applying his "Diet Evolution" principles and supplementing with coQ10 and niacin *(vitamin B3),* will help to lower the Lp(a) levels in most people by turning off the genes that produce them.

Understanding Triglycerides

"The level of triglycerides in each person's blood correlates exactly to his or her intake of "white," "beige," and "brown" foods, as well as of fruits."

- Dr. Steven Gundry

You lose weight as a result of falling triglyceride levels. Triglycerides fall when you shut off the body's mechanism for converting sugar to fat.

Some of The Most Problematic Foods

These foods should be avoided in order to aid in maintaining healthy triglyceride levels: ripe bananas, watermelon, honeydew, papayas, mangos, seedless grapes, ripe pears

The Myth of Whole Grains

Grains aren't entirely bad in whole form; but when processed, they invite the health issues we try to avoid. Grains are high in calories inherently. In the past grains helped us for survival when food was scarce. Processing them makes them easier to consume and digest, but doesn't leave us feeling full, which is why we are compelled to consume a lot of them; resulting in weight gain.

Understanding Fat

Fat is an essential nutrient in our diet, but its important to get the right kinds of fat.

The right kinds include:

- omega 3 fatty acids *(found in fish and flax)*

- fish and fish oil

- olives and olive oil

- avocados and avocado oil

- high ALA oils (walnut oil, canola oil, purslane oil, etc.)

NOTE: avoid artificial fats like trans fats (also known as hydrogenated oils) these do not activate the same receptors of fullness as do real fats.

<u>Tips for healthy fat consumption:</u>

- Look for green or brown colored oils

- Use oils on salads

- Pour oils on cooked vegetables

- Store oils in dark containers and/or refrigerate them to prevent premature rancidity

Grain Based Oils & Inflammation

Grain based oils contain a lot of omega 6. Omega 6 fatty acids are necessary but need to be balanced with omega 3 due to their inflammatory nature. Oils that are grain based tend to be beige.

Ex: corn, soybean, cottonseed, and safflower oil

NOTE: The Teardown phase helps you to get the omega 3 to 6 ratio back in check by staring clear of white and beige foods

Understanding Cravings

When omega 3s and 6s are in balance, sugar cravings tend to go down. Omega 3's also contain anti-depressant properties that might help reduce the desire to numb out by eating.

Added Supplementation

Supplementing with extracts in order to increase your antioxidant consumption is a viable alternative to consuming actual fruits Dr. Gundry suggests.

Here are a few extracts that he suggests:

- cranberry extract

- grape skin extract

- grape seed extract

- pycnogenols

- ALA

- mushroom extracts (like reishi, cordyceps, and maitake)

Hypertension

For treating hypertension, he recommends considering supplementing with hawthorne berries, olive leaf extract, magnesium, and manganese.

NOTE: These have properties that can help relax blood vessels

Fish Oil as a Supplement

Not all fish oil supplements are made equal. He recommends look for capsules and oils that are "molecularly distilled"

NOTE: Dr. Gundry recommends the Trader Joe's brand of fish oil.

Alternatives to fish oil include:

- flaxseed oil

- perilla oil

- hempseed oil

NOTE: supplementing with omega 3 can only do so much. Be sure to reduce your intake of omega 6's too.

Chapter 8 – Setting In

In chapter 8, Dr. Gundry warns us that we should anticipate a plateau in weight loss. He defines a plateau as 2 - 3 weeks of not losing weight.

Many people are tempted to quit when they encounter plateaus, but he recommends that you remind yourself of the other benefits of his protocol during those times:

• Decrease in total cholesterol of 50 points or so

• LDL ("bad") cholesterol tracking down

• HDL ("good") cholesterol tracking up

• Triglyceride level down

• Insulin level down

• Blood glucose level down

• Blood pressure down 10 to 20 points

• Percentage of body fat down

Why Plateaus Happen

Dr. Gundry says that we experience plateaus because we remove the food source of our fat cells.

Less fat = less burning of fat.

On average your weight x 10 calories is the amount your body needs to sustain its weight. In order to continue to lose weight, you have to adjust your food intake.

If and when you experience a plateau, continue following the Teardown phase. By doing this you reinforce your commitment to long term health by giving yourself the chance to practice avoiding the temptation to shift at signs of discomfort or not seeing progress.

Understanding Hunger

Ghrelin is a hormone that urges you to eat. Often periods of plateaus accompany an increase in ghrelin. Ghrelin increases in waves. Our genes responded to seasonal changes by encouraging us to eat more in summer and eat less in winter. By adhering to Dr. Gundry's regimen during times of increased ghrelin, you train your body to relax into the protocol. Consider limiting your intake of fruits and sleeping more to mimic the winter season.

How Sleep Affects Your Weight

Our ghrelin and leptin hormones regulate our weight. These hormones are sensitive to light and sleep length.

Leptin levels and ghrelin levels work inversely. The more sleep you get the less ghrelin *(hunger signals)* and more leptin *(fat burning signals)*. The less sleep you get the more ghrelin and less leptin.

Summer days tend to be longer and have more sun, while winter days tend to be shorter and have less sun. You can trick your genes to think its in the winter season by sleeping longer. This will then encourage your body to start burning stored fat for fuel.

Gaining Weight?

If you are gaining weight, you'll want to re-examine the foods in your diet and consider adjusting your portion sizes. Look to eliminate foods with sweet tastes and remember to avoid the beige and white foods in order to keep your triglycerides low.

Low triglycerides = weight loss

High triglycerides = weight gain

Dr. Gundry reminds us that it is possible to lose weight on those types of food in combination with fat restriction, but its not a long term solution because those foods will prevent your genes from registering that it is in a winter aka fat burning state.

If you are still not able to lose weight after verifying that you aren't consuming refined foods or excess fruits and grains, you then want to reduce your protein intake.

Supplements to Reduce Hunger & Cravings

St.John's Wort (300 mg - 3x a day)

SAM-e (200 mg on an empty stomach)

Citromax (500-1000 mg - 2x a day before lunch or dinner)

Understanding the Role of Exercise

Exercise helps to release pleasurable hormones like endorphins. These stress reducing hormones can be useful in adjusting to your new protocol.

NOTE: increasing muscle can prevent body size and/or weight reduction

Moving Past Phase 1

The decision to move to Phase 2 at this point is personal. If you continue to lose weight you've successfully communicated to your genes that they are in the "winter phase". If you have no health issues, you might want to consider moving on.

WARNINGS:

- if you still have insulin resistance or its almost gone, stay in the Teardown phase until you've lost at least 20 lbs.

- if you're LDL cholesterol levels have increased, you're part of a small group of people who respond poorly to a high protein higher animal fat diet. In this case, move on to the Restoration phase.

PHASE 2: The Restoration

Chapter 9 – The Beginning

In this phase we'll mimic the diet of our ancestors before agriculture and domestication *(about 10k year ago)*.

The human diet then was categorized as "calorie sparse", which research has shown is very effective for long term health and weight maintenance.

Understanding "Calorie Sparse" Compared to "Low Calorie"

The popular use of the term" low calorie" foods should not be confused with high quality foods low in calories *("calorie sparse)*.

"Low calorie" is often stamped on products used in marketing fad diets. These foods are often stripped of their nutrients, contains artificial ingredients, and are absent of the fiber necessary to trigger satiety.

Vegetables best fit the profile of high micro-nutrient and calorie sparse. Eating more micro-nutrients will help to increase your satisfaction without inducing the desire to indulge yourself.

Green leafy vegetables act as anti-hunger hormones because they quickly move to the lower intestines. The quicker food moves to the lower intestine the quicker you'll feel satiated.

Reducing High Calories Sources

Animal protein, cheese, grain, and legumes should all be reduced. The animal protein that helped ignite the transformation in the Teardown Phase will cease to be productive if we don't implement the Restoration phase.

NOTE: Its not so much about removal as it is getting the ratio of plants to animal protein and grains correct.

Less animal protein consumption has been linked to increased longevity due to less activation of certain "killer genes".

Why Animal Protein Long Term Is Harmful

Digesting animal protein requires your body to generate a lot of heat energy. Remember, your genes want to conserve energy and store fuel with the least amount of effort.

There is a misconception that we should seek to increase our heat energy and/or raise our metabolism, but we don't address the fact that this leads to the perception of inefficiency to our genes and thus the activation of certain "killer genes".

At first we want to use the heat from digesting animal protein to burn extra fat in the Teardown Phase, but then we want to quickly switch to slowing down the heat through the Restoration Phase for long term weight maintenance and health.

NOTE: The lower your metabolism is the less food you'll have to eat.

Dr. Gundry On Fat

Dr. Gundry suggests that while high fat diets can provide successful results early on, they should not be relied on in the long term. He references a study that targets long term successful dieters and noted that their diets were made up of 15% fat. These successful dieters were said to have the best control of their ghrelin levels.

Implementing the Restoration Phase

Remember these next 6 weeks that make up the Restoration phase is all about reducing your caloric density, and increasing the volume of calorie sparse foods. You'll continue eating the same types of foods, you'll just be focusing on adjusting the ratio.

Key features:

- bigger and varied vegetable portions

- large salads

- smaller portions of animal protein

- meat should be thought of as a side dish

Chapter 10 – Exercise

You can only lower your calories so much before feeling deprived, when you reach that point, that is where exercise comes in. Dr.Gundry purports that in the beginning phases of a diet, exercise does little to aid in long term weight loss. Exercise becomes necessary to sustain weight loss once you've gotten rid of your extra fat cells. Forming exercise habits that require you to "earn" extra food is a useful framework of mind.

Adopting A Walking Regimen

According to evolution we moved for 2 reasons: to find food and to avoid predators.

In this chapter, Dr. Gundry warns against prolonged running as a means for exercise, due to its extensive energy requirement. He advises that if you are going to run or walk for longer periods of time go slow. On the other hand, if you're going to run or walk for short periods of time, go fast.

Short fast durations promote muscle mass, while long durations promote catabolism.

Dr. Gundry recommends that you walk 10 - 20 minutes after eating; instead of before. When we eat before our meal, our body doesn't know when its next meal will be; as a result, it is encouraged to store fuel. If we've already eaten, our body is no longer concerned with satisfying its nutrition requirements, and can tap into its energy stores to burn fuel.

Weight Lifting

Dr. Gundry says that we should lift heavy and avoid excess repetitions like our ancestors did when they'd collect food and bring them back to their camp.

He suggests that the more we can mimic the actions of our ancestors, the more our genes will promote thriving. Following a weight lifting or bodyweight session with a small meal high in micro-nutrients helps to mimic our ancestors behaviors. In the inverse, the more we behave as though we are at threat through excessive running, excessive lifting, and eating micro-nutrient poor food, the more we activate our killer genes

Exercise & Insulin

Building muscle mass and reducing body fat helps to reduce insulin levels. Insulin is food for our muscles. As muscle decreases, our pancreas is forced to work harder to reduce insulin in the blood stream. Lower insulin levels also keeps the body from storing fat for future use.

Stimulating Muscle Growth With Supplementation

- CoQ10 - helps with muscle strength and stamina, and helps lower cholesterol

- Acetyl-L-carnitine or L-carnitine - transports energy to muscle cells

PHASE 3: Longevity

Chapter 11 – Raw Food Benefits

In phase 3 the focus turns from a general combination of cooked and raw foods to primarily raw foods. Dr. Gundry admits that this phase is not 100% necessary, but will provide you with steps to improve your quality of life and sustain your weight loss long term.

Raw foods preserves more micro-nutrients *(with some exceptions)*, and they contain more fiber, which helps to keep us full. He argues that our ancestors had to rely on plant protein most of the time and occasionally consumed animal protein when available.

Why Phase 3?

The objective of this phase is to lower your exposure to toxins in order to promote cell health.

NOTE: Mild exposure to stressors and toxins can provide benefits to our survival. Stressors like: mild exercise, heat, cold, fasting, uv light, etc.

Calorie Optimization

Calorie restriction acts as a mild stressor and as a result promotes the activation of health promoting genes.

NOTE: One study showed that Labrador retrievers lived 4 years longer when their calories were restricted by 25 percent.

Exposure to Plant Toxins

Vegetables do not promote cell growth. Research has shown that people who eat primarily vegetable diets tend to be short, have periods later, and live longer. This growth inhibition is believed to contribute to why young children and women during early phases of pregnancy tend to experience an aversion to plant consumption.

Our gene's attempts to battle plant toxins sends the message to our cells to conserve themselves instead of proliferate. This preservation helps to conserve energy and prevent the growth of cells that inhibit longevity.

Vegetables have hormetic characteristics. The more bitter, the more hormetic. In order to use foods for hormesis, start consuming more bitter vegetables like dandelion leaves, arugula, and watercress.

Stop Using The Stove

Heating foods reduces their micro-nutrients and their plant toxins.

NOTE: gradually transition to eating more raw foods in order to avoid symptoms experienced from a rush of plant toxins

Suggestions:

- start cooking your vegetables for a shorter duration

- snack on raw vegetables like string beans, broccoli, cauliflower, zucchini, sugar snap peas, celery, etc.

- incorporate more vegetables into your salads like beets, cauliflower, bell peppers, snow peas, etc.

- use shredded vegetables like cabbage, zucchini, and bean sprouts to replace noodles or rice.

- incorporate algaes and seaweeds and/or supplement with them *(ex: spirulina, chlorella, etc.)*

Chapter 12 – Beyond Diet

As the stress from eating lower calories results in the benefits of turning on health promoting genes, fasting can act as another practice to induce a healthy mild stressor.

Dr.Gundrys fasting tips:

- fast every other day

- skip meals periodically

On The Topic of Alcohol

Studies have shown that small amounts of alcohol can be beneficial in preventing illnesses like heart attacks. Of course in excess this is not the case.

The recommended daily limit is 2 servings for women and 2-3 for men. Alcohol has these protective properties because it stimulates blood vessels to manufacture a compound that works to dissolve blood clots and produce nitric oxide, which helps to keep blood vessels from constricting.

Coffee, Tea, & Chocolate

Chocolate in the form of 70% or greater of cocoa contains phytonutrients that helps to activate the sames genes that respond to plant toxins.

Drinking your coffee and tea without milk and other additives can help to preserve the phytonutrients found in those compounds. Many of the phytochemicals in tea and coffee are only able to be released in the presence of caffeine, so its important to avoid decaff unless you have medical issues that require you to do so.

NOTE: health issues do not tend to be observed in the consumption of coffee or tea up until 5 cups a day

Using Heat & Cold

Exposing your body to high temperatures activates heat-shock proteins. These proteins tells cells that aren't productive to self destruct.

Exposing your body to cold temperatures also activates genes that protect your longevity

Exercise

As we covered in the Restoration phase; while exercise is NOT an effective method to lose weight, it is effective for maintaining weight. Exercise activates hormesis, which helps to prolong life.

Word of Warning

Stress is good in moderation, but overdoing it will cause issues that can promote the activation of "killer genes".

Supplementation of Vitamins, Minerals, & Antioxidants

Supplementation with vitamins, minerals, and antioxidants have a limit. Research has shown that at certain doses these compounds can produce oxidative effects, which is exactly what we are looking to avoid in our pursuit of longevity.

Meal Implementation

Chapter 13 – Meal Plans & Recipes

The PDF meal plans included in the book can be found here:

http://content.randomhouse.com/assets/9780307409683/

For recipes from Dr.Gundry's plans, find them here:

https://gundrymd.com/category/dr-gundrys-recipes/

GIVEAWAY

I turned the friendly and unfriendly foods list from chapter 4 into a

PDF download for quick reference. You can print this list and

reference it when going grocery shopping or simply implementing

Dr.Gundry's dietary protocols at any point.

You can download the PDF here:

http://mindsetwarrior.com/diet-evolution-foods-optin

Conclusion

Overall, I enjoyed "Dr.Gundry's Diet Evolution". I really appreciate the understanding from a genetic level, and have yet to hear someone discuss diet and health so thoroughly from that angle. Dr. Gundry's protocol is one that I'm sure will work, I'm just not so sure that all the rules he outlines are necessary for high quality health. Even if you don't adopt all of its characteristics, I think understanding how your body responds to certain types of food is important when troubleshooting health or weight loss issues. I've done summaries on 2 other diet books that you might be interested in. I've summarized "The Complete Guide to Fasting" by Dr. Jason Fung and I've summarized "Fat for Fuel" by Dr. Joseph Mercola (you can find either summary @ http://mindsetwarrior.com/summary-guides)

Also don't forget to grab your friendly and unfriendly foods list here:

http://mindsetwarrior.com/diet-evolution-foods-optin

- Continue to the Next Page for Another Special Bonus -

BONUS:

Biases cloud our decision making on a day-to-day basis. You may have learned about a few of our cognitive biases back in your college or high school psychology class. It is time we get a refresher and understand how cognitive biases truly color our daily lives.

While we can't completely escape our biases, having an understanding of them can give us an advantage.

Get the FREE Cognitive Bias Report:

http://bit.ly/MWCogBiasReport

FEEDBACK:

If you'd like to provide feedback on how I can better improve these books, your opinion would be very much appreciated. Please send me an email at: summaries@mindsetwarrior.com I would love to hear from you.

- Alexa Taylor (The Mindset Warrior)

Made in the USA
Middletown, DE
14 February 2019